THIS COLORING BOOK BELONGS TO

____

Be Awesome
And
Give
No Fucks.

fucking
whore

Eat
A
Dick

Kick
ASS.

ZERO
FUCKS
GIVEN

be happy
it prives
assholes
crazy

NOT
GIVING
A FUCK
IS BETTER THAN
REVENGE

STOP
HARDING
EVERYTHING
ASSHOLE !

I googled
My
symptoms
Turns Out
I'm a Bitch.

Fresh
Out
Of
Fucks.

KEEP
CALM &
CARRY
THE F#CK
ON

You
are
Fucking
Magical

F#CKING
F#CK

SH#T
ARRIVED

BATSHIT
CRAZY

HAPPY
IT
DRIVES
ASSH#LES
CRAZY

BASIC
B#TCH

F#CK
INSANITY

LEAVE ME
THE F#CK
ALONE

YOU
LUCKY
BASTARD!

DO MORE
OF WHAT
MAKES YOU
F#CKING
HAPPY

FEELING
F#CKING
AWESOME

YOU
ARE
F#CKING
MAGICAL

YOU
F#CKING
GOT
THIS!

THIS
IS
BULLSHIT!

LOVE
F#CKING
WINE

KEEP CALM
AND DON'T
F#CK IT
UP

DO NO
HARM BUT
TAKE
NO SH!T

F#CKING
IDIOT

BE
F#CKING
FEARLESS

SUCH
A
P#SSY
SUCKER

YOU
SAVED
MY
ASS

SUCK
HIS
D!CK

ARE YOU F#CKING SERIOUS!

LET'S
F#CKING
DO
THIS!

OH, FOR F#CK'S SAKE!

CHOKE
ON MY
F#CKING
BALLS

KEEP
THAT
SH#T UP

THEY
MAY GO
FUCK
THEMSELVES

YOU
F#CKING
D#CKHEAD

SHUT
THE
F#CK
UP

WELL
SH#T

GET
THE
F#CK
OUT

F#CK
LET IT
BEEEE!

F#CKING
BULLSH#T

F#CK
IT LET'S
COLOR!

YES, I
F#CKING
CAN

FIND A
WAY NOT
A F#CKING
EXCUSE

A HEALTHY
MIND
IN A F#CKING
HEALTHY
TIME

NEVER
STOP
SH!TTY
DREAMING

Made in the USA
Las Vegas, NV
19 November 2024

12104092R00056